50 Ultimate Seafood Indulgence Recipes

By: Kelly Johnson

Table of Contents

- Lobster Thermidor
- Garlic Butter Lobster Tails
- Classic New England Clam Chowder
- Grilled Miso-Glazed Salmon
- Seafood Paella
- Butter Poached King Crab Legs
- Blackened Cajun Shrimp
- Creamy Lobster Mac & Cheese
- Smoked Salmon Eggs Benedict
- Shrimp Scampi with Linguine
- Seared Ahi Tuna with Sesame Crust
- Baked Oysters Rockefeller
- Garlic Butter Scallops
- Alaskan King Crab Bisque
- Caribbean Coconut Shrimp
- Cioppino Seafood Stew
- Charcoal-Grilled Prawns
- Thai Spicy Seafood Curry
- Honey Garlic Glazed Salmon
- Jumbo Lump Crab Cakes
- Tuna Tartare with Avocado
- Grilled Swordfish with Lemon Butter
- Tempura Fried Soft-Shell Crab
- Seafood Risotto with Saffron
- Baked Parmesan Crusted Halibut
- Lobster Ravioli in Creamy Tomato Sauce
- Clams in White Wine Garlic Sauce
- Smoked Trout Dip
- Lemon Herb Grilled Snapper
- Seafood Gumbo with Andouille Sausage
- Chilled Shrimp Cocktail
- Grilled Octopus with Lemon & Olive Oil
- Miso-Marinated Black Cod
- Spicy Tuna Poke Bowl
- Butterflied Garlic Prawns

- Spiny Lobster Tails with Citrus Butter
- Salt Crusted Branzino
- Sweet Chili Glazed Salmon
- Seafood-Stuffed Bell Peppers
- New Orleans BBQ Shrimp
- Pan-Seared Scallops with Truffle Oil
- Crab-Stuffed Mushrooms
- Crispy Beer-Battered Fish & Chips
- Sautéed Mussels in Spicy Tomato Broth
- Caviar & Crème Fraîche Blinis
- Baked Stuffed Lobster
- Grilled Mahi Mahi with Pineapple Salsa
- Creamy Garlic Butter Mussels
- Seafood-Stuffed Avocado Halves
- Clam & Chorizo Pasta

Lobster Thermidor

Ingredients:

- 2 lobster tails, cooked and meat removed
- 2 tbsp butter
- 1 shallot, minced
- 2 tbsp flour
- ½ cup white wine
- ½ cup heavy cream
- ½ cup Gruyère cheese, grated
- 1 tsp Dijon mustard
- Salt & pepper to taste

Instructions:

1. Sauté shallot in butter, add flour, and cook for 1 minute.
2. Stir in wine and cream, then add mustard, cheese, salt, and pepper.
3. Fold in lobster meat, then spoon back into shells.
4. Broil for 3-5 minutes until golden.

Garlic Butter Lobster Tails

Ingredients:

- 2 lobster tails, split in half
- 3 tbsp butter, melted
- 2 garlic cloves, minced
- 1 tsp lemon juice
- ½ tsp paprika
- Salt & pepper to taste

Instructions:

1. Mix butter, garlic, lemon juice, paprika, salt, and pepper.
2. Brush over lobster tails.
3. Broil for 8-10 minutes, basting with butter mixture.

Classic New England Clam Chowder

Ingredients:

- 200g clams, cleaned
- 2 tbsp butter
- 1 onion, diced
- 2 potatoes, diced
- 2 cups heavy cream
- 2 cups seafood stock
- ½ cup bacon, cooked and crumbled
- Salt & pepper to taste

Instructions:

1. Sauté onion in butter, add potatoes and stock, and simmer.
2. Stir in clams and cream. Cook until thickened.
3. Garnish with bacon.

Grilled Miso-Glazed Salmon

Ingredients:

- 2 salmon fillets
- 2 tbsp white miso paste
- 1 tbsp soy sauce
- 1 tbsp honey
- 1 tsp sesame oil

Instructions:

1. Mix miso, soy sauce, honey, and sesame oil.
2. Brush over salmon and marinate for 30 minutes.
3. Grill for 5 minutes per side.

Seafood Paella

Ingredients:

- 1 cup Arborio rice
- 2 cups seafood stock
- 200g mixed seafood (shrimp, mussels, squid)
- 1 onion, diced
- 1 bell pepper, diced
- 1 tsp smoked paprika
- ½ tsp saffron

Instructions:

1. Sauté onion and bell pepper. Stir in rice, saffron, and paprika.
2. Add stock and simmer for 15 minutes.
3. Stir in seafood and cook until done.

Butter Poached King Crab Legs

Ingredients:

- 500g king crab legs
- ½ cup butter, melted
- 1 garlic clove, minced
- 1 tsp lemon juice

Instructions:

1. Melt butter with garlic and lemon juice.
2. Poach crab legs in butter for 5 minutes.

Blackened Cajun Shrimp

Ingredients:

- 200g shrimp, peeled
- 1 tbsp Cajun seasoning
- 1 tbsp olive oil

Instructions:

1. Toss shrimp with seasoning and oil.
2. Sear in a hot pan for 2 minutes per side.

Creamy Lobster Mac & Cheese

Ingredients:

- 1 cup cooked lobster meat
- 2 cups macaroni
- 2 cups cheddar cheese, shredded
- 1 cup heavy cream
- 2 tbsp butter
- 1 tsp Dijon mustard

Instructions:

1. Cook macaroni, drain.
2. Melt butter, stir in cream, mustard, and cheese.
3. Add lobster and pasta, mix well.

Smoked Salmon Eggs Benedict

Ingredients:

- 2 poached eggs
- 2 English muffins, toasted
- 100g smoked salmon
- ½ cup hollandaise sauce

Instructions:

1. Top each muffin half with smoked salmon and poached egg.
2. Drizzle with hollandaise sauce.

Shrimp Scampi with Linguine

Ingredients:

- 200g shrimp, peeled
- 200g linguine
- 2 tbsp butter
- 2 garlic cloves, minced
- ½ cup white wine
- 1 tbsp lemon juice

Instructions:

1. Cook linguine, drain.
2. Sauté garlic in butter, add shrimp, wine, and lemon juice.
3. Toss with pasta.

Seared Ahi Tuna with Sesame Crust

Ingredients:

- 2 ahi tuna steaks
- 2 tbsp soy sauce
- 1 tbsp sesame oil
- 2 tbsp sesame seeds (black & white)
- 1 tsp grated ginger
- 1 tbsp vegetable oil

Instructions:

1. Marinate tuna in soy sauce, sesame oil, and ginger for 15 minutes.
2. Coat tuna with sesame seeds.
3. Heat oil in a pan and sear tuna for 1 minute per side.

Baked Oysters Rockefeller

Ingredients:

- 12 oysters, shucked
- 2 tbsp butter
- 1 shallot, minced
- 1 cup spinach, chopped
- ¼ cup breadcrumbs
- 2 tbsp Parmesan cheese
- 1 tbsp Pernod (optional)

Instructions:

1. Sauté shallot and spinach in butter. Add Pernod and cook for 1 minute.
2. Spoon mixture over oysters, top with breadcrumbs and cheese.
3. Bake at 400°F (200°C) for 10 minutes.

Garlic Butter Scallops

Ingredients:

- 200g scallops
- 2 tbsp butter
- 2 garlic cloves, minced
- 1 tbsp lemon juice
- Salt & pepper to taste

Instructions:

1. Heat butter in a pan, add garlic and sauté.
2. Sear scallops for 2 minutes per side.
3. Drizzle with lemon juice before serving.

Alaskan King Crab Bisque

Ingredients:

- 1 lb Alaskan king crab meat
- 2 tbsp butter
- 1 onion, chopped
- 2 garlic cloves, minced
- 2 tbsp flour
- 2 cups seafood stock
- 1 cup heavy cream
- Salt & pepper to taste

Instructions:

1. Sauté onion and garlic in butter. Add flour and cook for 1 minute.
2. Stir in stock and simmer.
3. Add crab meat and cream, cook for 5 minutes.

Caribbean Coconut Shrimp

Ingredients:

- 200g shrimp, peeled
- 1 cup shredded coconut
- ½ cup flour
- 1 egg, beaten
- ½ tsp paprika
- Oil for frying

Instructions:

1. Dredge shrimp in flour, dip in egg, and coat with coconut.
2. Fry in hot oil until golden.

Cioppino Seafood Stew

Ingredients:

- 200g mixed seafood (shrimp, mussels, clams, fish)
- 2 tbsp olive oil
- 1 onion, chopped
- 2 garlic cloves, minced
- 1 can diced tomatoes
- 2 cups seafood stock
- 1 tsp red pepper flakes

Instructions:

1. Sauté onion and garlic in olive oil.
2. Add tomatoes, stock, and red pepper flakes. Simmer for 10 minutes.
3. Stir in seafood and cook until done.

Charcoal-Grilled Prawns

Ingredients:

- 200g prawns, deveined
- 2 tbsp olive oil
- 1 tbsp lemon juice
- 1 tsp smoked paprika
- Salt & pepper to taste

Instructions:

1. Toss prawns in oil, lemon juice, paprika, salt, and pepper.
2. Grill over charcoal for 2 minutes per side.

Thai Spicy Seafood Curry

Ingredients:

- 200g mixed seafood
- 1 can coconut milk
- 2 tbsp red curry paste
- 1 bell pepper, sliced
- 1 tbsp fish sauce
- 1 tbsp lime juice

Instructions:

1. Sauté curry paste, add coconut milk and bring to a simmer.
2. Add seafood, bell pepper, fish sauce, and lime juice.
3. Cook until seafood is done.

Honey Garlic Glazed Salmon

Ingredients:

- 2 salmon fillets
- 2 tbsp honey
- 1 tbsp soy sauce
- 2 garlic cloves, minced
- 1 tbsp olive oil

Instructions:

1. Mix honey, soy sauce, and garlic.
2. Brush over salmon and bake at 375°F (190°C) for 12 minutes.

Jumbo Lump Crab Cakes

Ingredients:

- 1 lb jumbo lump crab meat
- ½ cup breadcrumbs
- 1 egg
- 2 tbsp mayonnaise
- 1 tsp Dijon mustard
- 1 tbsp lemon juice
- Salt & pepper to taste

Instructions:

1. Mix all ingredients, form into patties.
2. Sear in a pan for 3 minutes per side.

Tuna Tartare with Avocado

Ingredients:

- 200g sushi-grade tuna, diced
- 1 ripe avocado, diced
- 1 tbsp soy sauce
- 1 tsp sesame oil
- 1 tsp lime juice
- ½ tsp grated ginger
- 1 tbsp chopped chives
- Black sesame seeds for garnish

Instructions:

1. In a bowl, mix tuna, soy sauce, sesame oil, lime juice, and ginger.
2. Toss avocado with a bit of lime juice separately.
3. Layer avocado and tuna in a ring mold.
4. Garnish with chives and black sesame seeds.

Grilled Swordfish with Lemon Butter

Ingredients:

- 2 swordfish steaks
- 2 tbsp olive oil
- 1 tsp garlic powder
- Salt & pepper to taste
- 3 tbsp butter
- 1 tbsp lemon juice
- 1 tsp chopped parsley

Instructions:

1. Brush swordfish with olive oil, garlic powder, salt, and pepper.
2. Grill over medium heat for 4 minutes per side.
3. Melt butter in a pan, add lemon juice and parsley.
4. Drizzle over swordfish before serving.

Tempura Fried Soft-Shell Crab

Ingredients:

- 4 soft-shell crabs, cleaned
- 1 cup all-purpose flour
- 1 egg
- ¾ cup cold sparkling water
- 1 tsp salt
- Vegetable oil for frying

Instructions:

1. Whisk egg, flour, sparkling water, and salt into a batter.
2. Heat oil to 350°F (175°C).
3. Dip crabs into batter and fry for 3-4 minutes until golden.
4. Drain on paper towels and serve.

Seafood Risotto with Saffron

Ingredients:

- 1 cup Arborio rice
- 4 cups seafood stock
- ½ cup white wine
- 1 small onion, diced
- 1 garlic clove, minced
- 1 pinch saffron
- ½ lb mixed seafood (shrimp, scallops, mussels)
- 2 tbsp butter
- ¼ cup Parmesan cheese

Instructions:

1. Sauté onion and garlic in butter.
2. Add rice and toast for 1-2 minutes.
3. Deglaze with wine, then add saffron and warm stock gradually.
4. Stir constantly for 20 minutes until creamy.
5. Add seafood and cook for 3-4 minutes.
6. Stir in Parmesan and serve.

Baked Parmesan Crusted Halibut

Ingredients:

- 2 halibut fillets
- ½ cup grated Parmesan cheese
- ¼ cup breadcrumbs
- 1 tbsp olive oil
- 1 tsp lemon zest
- 1 tsp garlic powder
- Salt & pepper to taste

Instructions:

1. Preheat oven to 400°F (200°C).
2. Mix Parmesan, breadcrumbs, olive oil, lemon zest, garlic powder, salt, and pepper.
3. Coat halibut with the mixture.
4. Bake for 12-15 minutes until golden and flaky.

Lobster Ravioli in Creamy Tomato Sauce

Ingredients:

- 1 pack lobster ravioli
- 1 cup heavy cream
- ½ cup tomato sauce
- 2 tbsp butter
- 1 garlic clove, minced
- ¼ cup Parmesan cheese
- 1 tbsp fresh basil, chopped

Instructions:

1. Cook ravioli per package instructions.
2. Sauté garlic in butter, add tomato sauce and cream.
3. Simmer for 5 minutes, then stir in Parmesan.
4. Toss with ravioli and garnish with basil.

Clams in White Wine Garlic Sauce

Ingredients:

- 1 lb fresh clams
- 1 cup white wine
- 2 tbsp butter
- 2 garlic cloves, minced
- 1 tbsp lemon juice
- 1 tbsp parsley, chopped

Instructions:

1. Sauté garlic in butter.
2. Add clams and white wine, cover, and steam for 5-7 minutes.
3. Remove open clams and discard any that remain closed.
4. Stir in lemon juice and parsley, then serve.

Smoked Trout Dip

Ingredients:

- ½ lb smoked trout, flaked
- ½ cup cream cheese
- ¼ cup sour cream
- 1 tbsp lemon juice
- 1 tbsp fresh dill, chopped
- 1 tsp horseradish

Instructions:

1. Mix all ingredients in a bowl until smooth.
2. Chill for at least 30 minutes before serving.

Lemon Herb Grilled Snapper

Ingredients:

- 2 snapper fillets
- 2 tbsp olive oil
- 1 tbsp lemon juice
- 1 tsp garlic powder
- 1 tsp fresh thyme
- Salt & pepper to taste

Instructions:

1. Brush snapper with olive oil, lemon juice, garlic, thyme, salt, and pepper.
2. Grill for 3-4 minutes per side.

Seafood Gumbo with Andouille Sausage

Ingredients:

- ½ lb shrimp, peeled
- ½ lb crab meat
- 1 Andouille sausage, sliced
- 1 small onion, diced
- 1 bell pepper, diced
- 2 celery stalks, chopped
- 3 cups chicken broth
- 1 tbsp flour
- 1 tbsp butter
- 1 tsp Cajun seasoning

Instructions:

1. Sauté sausage, onion, bell pepper, and celery in butter.
2. Add flour and cook for 2 minutes.
3. Stir in broth, Cajun seasoning, and simmer for 15 minutes.
4. Add seafood and cook for 5 more minutes.

Chilled Shrimp Cocktail

Ingredients:

- ½ lb shrimp, cooked and chilled
- ½ cup cocktail sauce
- 1 tbsp lemon juice
- 1 tsp horseradish

Instructions:

1. Mix cocktail sauce with lemon juice and horseradish.
2. Serve with chilled shrimp.

Grilled Octopus with Lemon & Olive Oil

Ingredients:

- 1 whole octopus (about 2 lbs), cleaned
- 3 tbsp olive oil
- 2 tbsp lemon juice
- 2 garlic cloves, minced
- 1 tsp dried oregano
- Salt & pepper to taste

Instructions:

1. Bring a pot of salted water to a boil and simmer octopus for 45-60 minutes until tender.
2. Remove and let cool, then cut into pieces.
3. Toss with olive oil, lemon juice, garlic, oregano, salt, and pepper.
4. Grill over medium-high heat for 3-4 minutes per side.

Miso-Marinated Black Cod

Ingredients:

- 2 black cod fillets
- ¼ cup white miso paste
- 2 tbsp mirin
- 2 tbsp sake
- 1 tbsp sugar

Instructions:

1. Whisk together miso, mirin, sake, and sugar to make a marinade.
2. Coat cod and marinate for at least 4 hours or overnight.
3. Preheat oven to 400°F (200°C) and bake for 10-12 minutes until caramelized.

Spicy Tuna Poke Bowl

Ingredients:

- 200g sushi-grade tuna, diced
- 2 tbsp soy sauce
- 1 tsp sesame oil
- ½ tsp sriracha
- 1 tsp rice vinegar
- ½ cup cooked sushi rice
- ½ avocado, sliced
- ¼ cup cucumber, diced
- 1 tbsp sesame seeds
- 1 green onion, chopped

Instructions:

1. Mix tuna, soy sauce, sesame oil, sriracha, and rice vinegar.
2. Serve over sushi rice with avocado and cucumber.
3. Garnish with sesame seeds and green onions.

Butterflied Garlic Prawns

Ingredients:

- 1 lb large prawns, butterflied
- 3 tbsp butter, melted
- 3 garlic cloves, minced
- 1 tbsp lemon juice
- 1 tsp paprika
- Salt & pepper to taste

Instructions:

1. Preheat oven to 400°F (200°C).
2. Arrange prawns on a baking sheet.
3. Mix butter, garlic, lemon juice, paprika, salt, and pepper.
4. Brush prawns with mixture and bake for 8-10 minutes.

Spiny Lobster Tails with Citrus Butter

Ingredients:

- 2 spiny lobster tails
- 4 tbsp butter, melted
- 1 tbsp orange juice
- 1 tbsp lemon juice
- 1 garlic clove, minced
- Salt & pepper to taste

Instructions:

1. Preheat grill to medium-high.
2. Mix butter, orange juice, lemon juice, garlic, salt, and pepper.
3. Split lobster tails in half and brush with butter mixture.
4. Grill for 5-7 minutes per side.

Salt Crusted Branzino

Ingredients:

- 1 whole branzino, cleaned
- 4 cups coarse sea salt
- 2 egg whites
- 1 lemon, sliced
- 2 sprigs rosemary

Instructions:

1. Preheat oven to 400°F (200°C).
2. Stuff fish with lemon slices and rosemary.
3. Mix salt and egg whites, then coat fish completely.
4. Bake for 25-30 minutes, then crack open salt crust to serve.

Sweet Chili Glazed Salmon

Ingredients:

- 2 salmon fillets
- 3 tbsp sweet chili sauce
- 1 tbsp soy sauce
- 1 tbsp lime juice
- 1 tsp grated ginger

Instructions:

1. Mix sweet chili sauce, soy sauce, lime juice, and ginger.
2. Coat salmon and marinate for 30 minutes.
3. Bake at 400°F (200°C) for 12-15 minutes.

Seafood-Stuffed Bell Peppers

Ingredients:

- 4 bell peppers, halved and deseeded
- ½ lb shrimp, chopped
- ½ lb crab meat
- ½ cup cooked rice
- ¼ cup diced onion
- 2 garlic cloves, minced
- 1 tsp Old Bay seasoning
- ½ cup shredded cheese

Instructions:

1. Preheat oven to 375°F (190°C).
2. Sauté onion and garlic, then mix with shrimp, crab, rice, and seasoning.
3. Stuff peppers, top with cheese, and bake for 20 minutes.

New Orleans BBQ Shrimp

Ingredients:

- 1 lb large shrimp, shell on
- 4 tbsp butter
- 2 garlic cloves, minced
- 1 tbsp Worcestershire sauce
- 1 tbsp hot sauce
- ½ tsp smoked paprika
- ½ tsp cayenne pepper
- Juice of 1 lemon

Instructions:

1. Melt butter in a pan and sauté garlic.
2. Add Worcestershire, hot sauce, paprika, and cayenne.
3. Toss in shrimp and cook for 3-4 minutes.
4. Finish with lemon juice and serve.

Pan-Seared Scallops with Truffle Oil

Ingredients:

- 8 large sea scallops
- 2 tbsp olive oil
- 1 tbsp butter
- Salt & pepper to taste
- 1 tbsp truffle oil
- 1 tbsp chopped parsley

Instructions:

1. Pat scallops dry and season with salt and pepper.
2. Heat olive oil in a pan over medium-high heat.
3. Sear scallops for 2-3 minutes per side until golden brown.
4. Remove from heat, drizzle with truffle oil, and garnish with parsley.

Crab-Stuffed Mushrooms

Ingredients:

- 12 large mushrooms, stems removed
- ½ cup crab meat
- ¼ cup cream cheese, softened
- 2 tbsp mayonnaise
- 1 garlic clove, minced
- 2 tbsp Parmesan cheese
- 1 tsp lemon juice
- Salt & pepper to taste

Instructions:

1. Preheat oven to 375°F (190°C).
2. Mix crab meat, cream cheese, mayonnaise, garlic, Parmesan, lemon juice, salt, and pepper.
3. Fill mushrooms with the mixture and bake for 15-20 minutes.

Crispy Beer-Battered Fish & Chips

Ingredients:

- 4 cod fillets
- 1 cup flour
- ½ cup cornstarch
- 1 tsp baking powder
- 1 tsp salt
- 1 cup beer (cold)
- Oil for frying
- 4 large potatoes, cut into fries

Instructions:

1. Heat oil to 375°F (190°C).
2. Mix flour, cornstarch, baking powder, and salt. Slowly whisk in beer.
3. Dip fish in batter and fry for 5-7 minutes until golden.
4. Fry potatoes until crispy. Serve with tartar sauce.

Sautéed Mussels in Spicy Tomato Broth

Ingredients:

- 2 lbs mussels, cleaned
- 2 tbsp olive oil
- 1 onion, chopped
- 2 garlic cloves, minced
- 1 can diced tomatoes (14 oz)
- 1 tsp red pepper flakes
- ½ cup white wine
- Salt & pepper to taste
- Fresh parsley for garnish

Instructions:

1. Heat oil in a large pan. Sauté onion and garlic.
2. Add tomatoes, red pepper flakes, white wine, salt, and pepper. Simmer for 10 minutes.
3. Add mussels, cover, and cook for 5 minutes until mussels open. Garnish with parsley.

Caviar & Crème Fraîche Blinis

Ingredients:

- 1 cup flour
- 1 tsp baking powder
- 1 cup buttermilk
- 1 egg
- 1 tbsp butter, melted
- ½ cup crème fraîche
- 2 oz caviar
- Chives for garnish

Instructions:

1. Mix flour and baking powder. Whisk in buttermilk, egg, and butter.
2. Cook small pancakes in a skillet over medium heat.
3. Top with crème fraîche, caviar, and chives.

Baked Stuffed Lobster

Ingredients:

- 2 whole lobsters, split in half
- ½ cup crab meat
- ¼ cup breadcrumbs
- 2 tbsp butter, melted
- 1 tbsp lemon juice
- 1 garlic clove, minced
- Salt & pepper to taste

Instructions:

1. Preheat oven to 375°F (190°C).
2. Mix crab meat, breadcrumbs, butter, lemon juice, garlic, salt, and pepper.
3. Stuff lobster halves and bake for 15-20 minutes.

Grilled Mahi Mahi with Pineapple Salsa

Ingredients:

- 2 Mahi Mahi fillets
- 1 tbsp olive oil
- Salt & pepper to taste
- 1 cup pineapple, diced
- ¼ cup red onion, chopped
- 1 tbsp lime juice
- 1 tbsp cilantro, chopped

Instructions:

1. Preheat grill to medium-high heat.
2. Brush fish with olive oil, season with salt and pepper.
3. Grill for 4-5 minutes per side.
4. Mix pineapple, onion, lime juice, and cilantro for salsa. Serve over fish.

Creamy Garlic Butter Mussels

Ingredients:

- 2 lbs mussels, cleaned
- 2 tbsp butter
- 4 garlic cloves, minced
- ½ cup heavy cream
- ½ cup white wine
- Salt & pepper to taste
- Fresh parsley for garnish

Instructions:

1. Melt butter in a pan, sauté garlic for 1 minute.
2. Add wine and mussels, cover, and cook for 5 minutes.
3. Stir in cream, season with salt and pepper, and simmer for 2 minutes.
4. Garnish with parsley and serve.

Seafood-Stuffed Avocado Halves

Ingredients:

- 2 avocados, halved
- ½ cup shrimp, cooked & chopped
- ¼ cup crab meat
- 2 tbsp mayonnaise
- 1 tbsp lemon juice
- Salt & pepper to taste
- Paprika for garnish

Instructions:

1. Scoop out some avocado flesh, mix with shrimp, crab, mayo, lemon juice, salt, and pepper.
2. Fill avocado halves with the mixture. Sprinkle with paprika.

Clam & Chorizo Pasta

Ingredients:

- 8 oz spaghetti
- 1 lb fresh clams, cleaned
- 4 oz chorizo, sliced
- 2 garlic cloves, minced
- ½ cup white wine
- 2 tbsp olive oil
- Salt & pepper to taste
- Fresh parsley for garnish

Instructions:

1. Cook spaghetti according to package instructions.
2. Heat oil in a pan, cook chorizo until crispy.
3. Add garlic and clams, then pour in wine. Cover and cook for 5 minutes until clams open.
4. Toss with pasta and garnish with parsley.

www.ingramcontent.com/pod-product-compliance
Lightning Source LLC
LaVergne TN
LVHW081506060526
838201LV00056BA/2967